HOW DID WE FIND OUT
ABOUT BLACK HOLES?

The "HOW DID WE FIND OUT . . . ?" SERIES
by Isaac Asimov

HOW DID WE FIND OUT

ABOUT BLACK HOLES?

Isaac Asimov
Illustrated by David Wool

WALKER AND COMPANY
New York

Asimov, Isaac, 1920–
    How did we find out about black holes?

    (How did we find out books)
    Includes index.
    SUMMARY: Discusses why scientists believe in the
existence of black holes, what they are, how they are
formed, and how they are detected.
    1. Black holes (Astronomy)—Juvenile literature.
[1. Black holes (Astronomy)] I. Title.
QB843.B55A85   523.8   78–4320
ISBN 0–8027–6336–7
ISBN 0–8027–6337–5 lib. bdg.

Text Copyright © 1978 by Isaac Asimov
Illustrations Copyright © 1978 by David Wool

First published in the United States of America
in 1978 by the Walker Publishing Company, Inc.

Published simultaneously in Canada by Thomas Allen & Sons
Canada, Limited, Markham, Ontario.

TRADE ISBN: 0-8027-6336-7
REINF. ISBN: 0-8027-6337-5

Library of Congress Catalog Card Number: 78-4320

Printed in the United States of America

10 9 8

To Barton Behr, who helps make life interesting

Contents

1 White Dwarfs

IN 1844 A GERMAN astronomer, Friedrich Wilhelm Bessel (BES-ul), discovered a star he couldn't see.

This is how it happened.

All the stars we see in the sky are moving about. They are so far away from us, though, that the motion seems very slow indeed. Only by making careful measurements through the telescope will the motion show up as very tiny changes in position.

Even using the telescope won't help much. Only the nearest stars show changes in position when compared with dim, distant stars so far away that they don't seem to move at all.

One of the stars nearest to us is Sirius (SIR-ee-us.) It is about 50 trillion miles away, but that is close for a star. It is the brightest star in the sky, partly because it is so close, and its motion can be measured easily through a telescope.

Friedrich Bessel

Bessel wanted to study that motion carefully, because as the earth goes around the sun, we keep seeing the stars from slightly different angles. Instead of seeing a star move in a straight line, we see it move in a line that wiggles slightly because of the earth's motion.

The nearer the star, the larger the wiggle. From the size of the wiggle, if it is carefully measured, the distance of a star can be calculated. Bessel was particularly interested in this. In fact, he was the first astronomer ever to calculate the distance of a star. He did that in 1838.

He then became interested in measuring the wiggle in Sirius's motion. As he measured the position of Sirius night after night for a long time, he found that there was more of a wiggle to its motion than he had expected. It changed position because the earth was revolving around the sun, but there was another change in position too—a slower one that had nothing to do with the earth.

Bessel concentrated on this new movement and found that Sirius was moving in an orbit around something or other, just the way the earth moves in an orbit about the sun. He calculated that it would take Sirius fifty years to complete its orbit.

But what caused Sirius to move in this orbit?

The earth moves about the sun because it is held by the sun's powerful gravitational pull. Sirius must be held in a powerful gravitational pull of some sort too.

Sirius, however, is a star that has two and a half times the mass of our sun. (*Mass* is the amount of matter something contains.)

11

From the way in which Sirius was moving, it had to be feeling the gravitational pull of a body that was large enough to be a star also. In other words, Sirius and a companion star had to be circling each other. We might call Sirius "Sirius A" and its companion star "Sirius B."

From the way in which Sirius A was moving, its companion star, Sirius B, had to be just about exactly as massive as our sun.

Yet Bessel couldn't see Sirius B. It had to be there, for the gravitational pull had to come from something.

Bessel decided, therefore, that Sirius B was a star that had burnt to a cinder that no longer shone and therefore could not be seen. He called it the *dark companion* of Sirius.

Later on, he noticed that the star Procyon (PROH-see-on) moved in such a way that it must also have a dark companion, "Procyon B."

Bessel had discovered *two* stars he couldn't see.

In 1862 an American telescope maker, Alvan Graham Clark, was making a lens for a new telescope. Such a lens must be polished perfectly so that stars can be seen sharply through it.

When he was finished, he tested the lens by looking through it at the star Sirius to see if it would show up as a sharp point of light.

When he did so, he was surprised to find that there was a dim spark of light near Sirius. If this was a star, it was not on any of the star maps that he had. Maybe it was the result of a flaw in the polishing of the lens.

No matter how carefully he continued to polish the lens, though, that spark of light did not go away. And there was no similar spark when he looked at any other bright star.

Finally, Clark noticed that the spark of light was in just the position that Sirius's dark companion ought to be, and he knew he was looking at it.

Sirius B was not a completely dead star after all. It still shone, but with only $\frac{1}{10000}$ the light of Sirius A.

In 1895 a German-American astronomer, John Martin Schaeberle (SHAY-ber-lee), noticed a dim spark of light near Procyon. It was Procyon B, and it wasn't completely dead either.

By Schaeberle's time, though, astronomers had learned more about stars.

Light consists of tiny waves of different lengths, and astronomers had learned to separate starlight into a spread of these different wavelengths. Such a spread is called a *spectrum* (SPEK-trum).

In 1893 a German scientist, Wilhelm Wien (VEEN), showed how a spectrum changed with

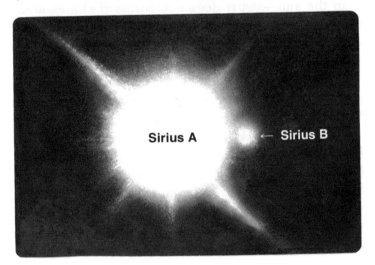

White dwarf

Sun at present

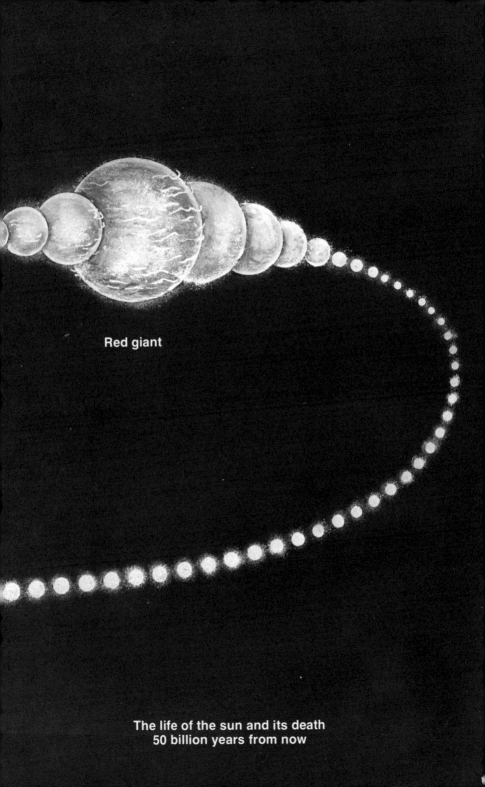

Red giant

The life of the sun and its death
50 billion years from now

stronger. Atoms at the center of a star have smashed electron shells. The electrons then move about loosely and do not surround the nuclei.

As a result, the nuclei can move about freely. They can even bump together and stick, thus undergoing changes that produce energy. So much energy is produced that the center of a star can have a temperature of several million degrees. Some of that heat leaks out of the surface of the star in all directions, and that is why the star shines as it does. The heat developed in this way keeps the star expanded and doesn't let the atoms smash except at the very center.

The energy at the center of a star comes from the changeover of hydrogen nuclei (the smallest there are) to helium nuclei (the next smallest). Eventually, though, most of the hydrogen in the star is used up.

But by that time the center has become so hot that the added heat causes the star to expand into a giant star. The surface of the star cools as this happens and turns red, which is why such a star is called a *red giant*.

When the hydrogen is nearly all gone, the thin, outermost layers of the star expand away into a gas and finally disappear, but the inner layers, with almost all the mass of the star, now have no more energy to keep them hot. Gravity pulls those layers quickly inward, and the star collapses. It collapses so quickly and gravity pulls so hard that just about all the electron shells collapse, and all the nuclei will come much closer together than they would in ordinary stars.

The star then has its mass squeezed into a small volume. It has become a white dwarf.

In the case of the sun, this will not happen for about five billion years. It has already happened, though, to some stars that have run out of their hydrogen fuel. Sirius B and Procyon B are examples of this.

2 Limits and Explosions

GRAVITATIONAL PULL is stronger as you get closer to the center of any object, provided all the mass stays between you and the center.

Imagine yourself standing on the sun. The gravitational pull on you would be 28 times what it is on the earth. If all the mass of the sun were packed more and more tightly together and you still stayed on the surface, which would be contracting, you would get closer and closer to the center and the gravitational pull on you would be stronger and stronger.

On the sun's surface as it is, you are 432,000 miles from its center. On the surface of Sirius B there would be the same mass under you, but you would be only 15,000 miles from the center. If you were standing on the surface of Sirius B, the gravitational pull on you would be 840 times what it would be if you were on the surface of the sun, and 23,500 times

Albert Einstein

what it would be if you were back on earth.

How do we check this? Can we tell whether Sirius B really has such an enormous surface gravity?

In 1915 a German-Swiss scientist, Albert Einstein, worked out a new theory of gravitation. According to this theory, when light moves outward against a gravitational pull, all its wavelengths become a little longer. The stronger the gravitational pull, the longer the wavelengths.

The longest waves of light we can see are those of red light. This means that when light waves become longer, they seem to become redder—that is, they shift toward the red end of the spectrum. Einstein predicted a gravitational *red shift*.

Although the sun's gravitational pull is much stronger than the earth's, it is still not strong enough to do more than produce a very small red shift. That red shift is too small to measure accurately. But what about Sirius B, with its very strong gravitational pull?

In 1925 Adams, who had first studied the spectrum of Sirius B, did so again. He found that there *was* a red shift in the spectrum, just as Einstein's theory had predicted. Sirius B *did* have an enormous gravitational field.

That was the final proof that Sirius B was small and very dense. And, of course, if that was what Sirius B was like, that was what all white dwarfs would be like. Our sun will be like that someday in the far, far future.

But if gravitational pull becomes stronger and stronger as a star collapses, what stops the collapse and forms a white dwarf? Why doesn't the star collapse all the way?

Even after atoms have broken down and the electron shells are smashed, the electrons themselves still exist. They take up much more room than the nuclei do, and they keep the white dwarf from shrinking further.

The more massive a star is, however, the stronger its gravitational pull and the more tightly its matter is forced together. A white dwarf that is more massive than Sirius B would pull itself together more tightly and be smaller than Sirius B.

What happens if a white dwarf is very massive?

In 1931 an Indian-American astronomer, Subrahmanyan Chandrasekhar (soob-rah-MAHN-yahn chan-druh-SEEK-har), studied this question. He was able to show that if a white dwarf were massive enough, it would force its way through the resistance of the electrons and collapse further.

He figured out just how massive a white dwarf

Subrahmanyan Chandrasekhar

would have to be in order to collapse further. It would have to be 1.4 times as massive as our sun. That is called *Chandrasekhar's limit.*

The white dwarfs that astronomers have found and studied so far all have masses that are less than Chandrasekhar's limit.

This raises a problem.

If all stars are less than 1.4 times the mass of our sun to begin with, then everything would be easily explained. The stars would all eventually become white dwarfs just as our own sun will.

The trouble is that some stars have more mass than that. About 2.5 percent of all the stars in the sky are more than 1.4 times as massive as the sun. That doesn't sound like much, but there are so many stars altogether that even 2.5 percent of them are a large number.

The stars in the universe are collected into large groups called *galaxies* (GAL-ak-seez). Our own galaxy is made up of about 120 billion stars. That means there are about three billion stars alone in our own galaxy with masses that are over Chandrasekhar's limit. A few are even as much as sixty or seventy times as massive as our sun.

What happens to them?

When astronomers studied massive stars, they found that the more massive a star, the shorter and stormier its life.

The more massive a star, the more tightly its gravity pulls it together and the hotter it must be to keep it from collapsing. The hotter it is, the more rapidly it uses up its hydrogen fuel. For that reason a massive star has a shorter lifetime than a less massive star.

It takes a star as massive as the sun 10 billion years to use up its fuel, but a star three times as massive as the sun will use up its fuel in only half a billion years. That is one reason that there are so few really massive stars. They do not last long.

Besides, the more massive a star is, the larger it expands when it becomes a red giant, and the more

Different sizes of stars of the same mass

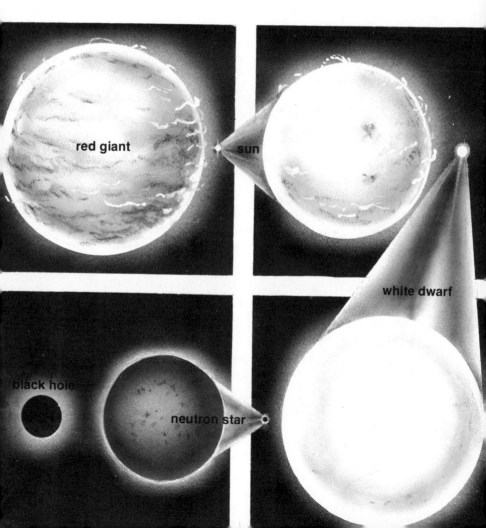

suddenly it collapses when the fuel is finally used up.

When a star collapses suddenly enough, it explodes in the process. The more massive it is, the greater the explosion.

When a star explodes, it uses up all the hydrogen fuel still left in its outer layers. It does this very rapidly and the star glows up to 100 billion times as brightly as it did before, and it may keep on doing so for a few weeks.

Sometimes a dim star, one that is too dim to see without a telescope, becomes so bright it can be seen. To the astronomers before the invention of the telescope, it seemed that a new star had appeared in the sky. It was therefore called a *nova* (NOH-vuh), from a Latin word for "new."

Some novas don't become very bright and are the result of matter from another star falling upon them and glowing. Very bright novas result from actual explosions of massive stars and are now called *supernovas*.

This seemed a possible way out of the difficulty of Chandrasekhar's limit. When a star turns into a supernova, the explosion hurls much of the matter in the star off into outer space. Only a small part of it hangs together and collapses.

Perhaps, when a massive star explodes, so much matter is hurled into outer space that the part that collapses is always less massive than Chandrasekhar's limit.

If so, that would mean it was possible that all stars, however massive they might be to begin with, would eventually turn into not so massive white dwarfs.

3 Pulsars and Neutron Stars

NOT ALL ASTRONOMERS were certain that supernovas were a sure way around Chandrasekhar's limit.

Some of them kept thinking about what might happen when a giant star exploded. It seemed to them that only a certain part of its mass could be thrown into space, and that might not be enough to bring it below Chandrasekhar's limit. In fact, it seemed to them a star couldn't possibly lose more than 90 percent of its mass in a supernova explosion. If so, a star that was more than fifteen times as massive as the sun was sure to end up with a collapsing mass that was greater than Chandrasekhar's limit.

Besides, with massive stars, collapse could be so sudden that even if the mass of the collapsing part were less than Chandrasekhar's limit, the electrons might be smashed as the star squeezed together. What would happen then?

Fritz Zwicky   **Walter Baade**

In 1934 the Swiss-American astronomer Fritz Zwicky (TSVIK-ee) and the German-American astronomer Walter Baade (BAH-duh) puzzled over this question, and this is the way it seemed to them:

The nucleus in the atom is made up of two kinds of particles—*protons* (PROH-tonz) and *neutrons* (NOO-tronz). They are very much alike, except that each proton has an electric charge whereas each neutron has none.

The electrons that exist outside the nucleus in ordinary atoms, and even in the smashed atoms of a white dwarf, also carry an electric charge. The electric charge on the electron is exactly the same size as that on the proton, but the two charges are of opposite kinds. The electric charge on the proton is called *positive*, and the one on the electron is *negative*.

If an electron and a proton are forced together and

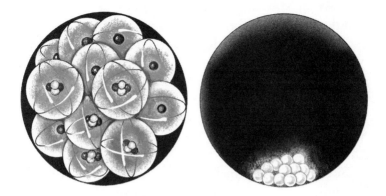

Collapse of atoms

made to join, the two opposite electric charges cancel each other. What is left is a neutron, with no charge.

Zwicky and Baade felt that if the mass of a collapsing star were greater than Chandrasekhar's limit, or if the collapse itself were rapid enough, all the electrons would then be forced into the nucleus. The protons in the nucleus would become neutrons, and the collapsing star would then consist of nothing but neutrons.

With all the electrons gone, there would be nothing to keep the neutrons from coming closer and closer to each other until they touched. The collapsing mass would then become a *neutron star*.

Neutrons are so much smaller than atoms that a neutron star would be tiny. The sun, for instance, is a big ball of hot gas 864,000 miles across. If all its electrons and protons were turned into neutrons, and it shrank till all its neutrons touched, it would become a neutron star not quite nine miles across. But it would still have all the original mass of the sun.

To Zwicky and Baade it seemed that white dwarfs would form only from stars that were too small to explode as supernovas. Stars large enough to go through a supernova stage would collapse to neutron stars. (Our sun is too small to explode. Some day it will collapse to a white dwarf, but not to a neutron star.)

But if a neutron star is only a few miles in diameter, how can we ever check the theory and find out if Zwicky and Baade are right? Surely even the best telescope wouldn't show us a tiny ball only a few miles in diameter when it is trillions of miles away from us.

Perhaps there is a way out. If a huge star collapses into a neutron star, the energy of collapse turns to heat. The surface of the neutron star should be at a temperature of 10 million degrees. That is almost as hot as the center of our sun.

A surface that has a temperature of 10 million degrees is too hot to give off much in the way of ordinary light. It gives off radiation that is like light but much more energetic. The more energetic such radiation is, the shorter its waves are, so the radiation given off by neutron stars consists of very short waves indeed. Such short-wave radiation is called X *rays.*

A neutron star should give off waves of all lengths, including those of ordinary light, and of radiation with still longer wavelength, such as radio waves. It should certainly give off X rays.

If we could study X rays coming from different places in the sky, then we could tell whether there are neutron stars somewhere out in space. One trouble, though, is that X rays can't get through the atmosphere. Ordinary light can, but X rays cannot.

Fortunately, beginning in the 1950s, scientists were able to send rockets into space beyond the atmosphere. Instruments carried by those rockets can study radiation from the sky before it reaches the atmosphere.

In 1963, under the direction of the American astronomer Herbert Friedman, rockets were sent out carrying instruments that could detect X rays. X rays were indeed found to come from different places in the sky, but were they coming from neutron stars or from other objects?

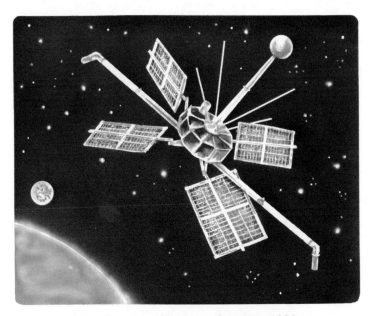

Interplanetary Explorer Satellite 1963
based on NASA photo

One of the places from which X rays were coming was the "Crab Nebula." The Crab Nebula is a patch of dust and gas; it is all that remains of a gigantic supernova that exploded in the year 1054. Could there be a neutron star in the middle of it?

That was hard to say. The X rays might be coming from the hot dust and gas—that is, there might be no neutron star at all.

In 1964 the moon happened to pass in front of the Crab Nebula. If the X rays were coming from the dust and gas, it would take a while for the moon to cover it all, and the X rays would be cut off little by little. If the X rays were coming from a tiny neutron star, the moon would pass in front of it almost in no time, and the X rays would be cut off all at once.

The X rays were cut off little by little, and it seemed that there was no neutron star there.

However, that wasn't the end of the story. In 1931 an American engineer, Karl Jansky, had discovered that there were radio waves coming from the sky. Radio waves are like light waves except that they are much longer. Certain kinds of radio waves can get through the atmosphere as easily as light waves can, and these were what Jansky had detected.

In the 1950s astronomers built special instruments called *radio telescopes* to catch these radio waves and study them.

By the early 1960s it seemed to some astronomers that in some cases the radio waves grew stronger and weaker very quickly. They seemed to be doing so more rapidly than the radio telescopes could catch the changes.

In 1967 a British astronomer, Anthony Hewish,

Jocelyn Bell and Cambridge Radio Telescope

had built a special radio telescope that would catch those very rapid changes.

It was set to work in July 1967, and within a month one of Hewish's students, Jocelyn Bell, was catching short bursts or *pulses* of radio waves from a particular place in the sky. Each pulse lasted only one-twentieth of a second, and came regularly every 1.33730109 seconds. They never vary in their timing by even as much as a hundred-millionth of a second.

Hewish and Bell looked elsewhere in the skies and soon found three more places where rapid pulses of radio waves could be found. Each one had a different period, of course. Naturally, they didn't know what produced these pulses, so they just called them *pulsating stars.* This was soon shortened to *pulsars.*

Other astronomers also located pulsars. In ten years over a hundred were found. There may be 100,000 of them in our galaxy altogether.

A pulsar located in the Crab Nebula has the shortest period yet found. The pulses come every 0.033099 seconds. That means one pulse every thirtieth of a second.

The Austrian-born astronomer Thomas Gold felt that in order to produce such pulses, some object in space must be going through some change very regularly and very rapidly. Two objects might be revolving about each other, or one object might be expanding and contracting or spinning on its axis.

There was a problem, though. To produce radio waves strong enough to be detected across distances

Crab Nebula

of trillions of miles, an object would have to be as massive as a star.

But ordinary stars couldn't move fast enough. Stars couldn't revolve about each other every second, or expand and contract every second, or rotate every second. Stars trying to move that quickly would tear apart. In order to undergo such rapid changes, an object would have to be much smaller than a star and would have to have a much stronger gravitational pull holding it together. Even white dwarfs wouldn't be small enough and wouldn't be held together by enough gravitational pull.

What about a neutron star? Gold decided that it had to be the answer. A neutron star is so small and has such a strong gravitational pull that it can turn on its axis in a second, or even in a thirtieth of a second without breaking apart.

Gold suggested that the radio waves might only come out of certain spots on the neutron star's surface. Each time the neutron star turned, a spray of radio waves would sweep out in our direction.

Gold also decided that as the neutron star sent out radiation, it would lose energy. Its rate of rotation should therefore slow down very gradually.

The pulsar in the Crab Nebula, for instance, has such a rapid period because the neutron star only formed about a thousand years ago and is the youngest we know of. It hasn't had time to slow down much, but it should still be slowing down.

The pulsar in the Crab Nebula was studied carefully, and Gold turned out to be right. Its period is getting very slightly longer each day. Each day the period is 36 billionths of a second longer than it was the day before.

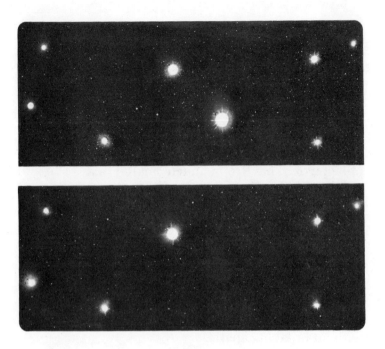

Pulsar in Crab Nebula

Flashing on (top)   and off (bottom)

Astronomers have pretty well decided now that pulsars are indeed rotating neutron stars.

Of course, a rotating neutron star should be sending out all kinds of radiation, not just radio waves. The other kinds of radiation should also be reaching us in pulses.

For instance, the Crab Nebula neutron star sends out pulses of X rays, too. About an eighth of the Crab Nebula's X rays come from the neutron star. The remaining seven-eighths come from the surrounding dust and gas produced by the supernova. That seven-eighths is what made it look as though there were no neutron star there when the moon passed in front of the Crab Nebula.

A rotating neutron star should also send out pulses of light. In January 1969, a very dim star inside the Crab Nebula was found to be going on and off thirty times a second. It was sending out pulses of light. It was the actual neutron star and astronomers could see it.

A second neutron star, in the debris of another supernova, has since been seen. This second neutron star is named "Vela X-1" (VEE-luh) because it is in the constellation Vela, the Sails.

In 1975, the mass of Vela X-1 was measured. It was found to have a mass 1.5 times that of the sun.

The mass of Vela X-1 is over Chandrasekhar's limit. That is another piece of evidence in favor of its being a neutron star. An object with the mass of Vela X-1 couldn't possibly be a white dwarf.

4 Escape Velocity and Tides

A WHITE DWARF may be very dense and may have a very strong gravitational pull, but a neutron star is far denser and has a far stronger pull.

Earlier in the book, I said that a cubic inch of material from Sirius B would have a mass of 1,250 pounds. Suppose that, instead, we considered a cubic inch of matter from a neutron star with a mass equal to that of the sun or of Sirius B. That cubic inch would have a mass of 25 billion tons. A cubic mile of material from the neutron star would have a mass a thousand times as great as that of the whole earth.

Suppose you weigh 100 pounds. If you could somehow imagine yourself to be standing on the sun, you would weigh 2,800 pounds, or nearly 1.5 tons. On Sirius B you would weigh 1,050 tons.

On a neutron star with the mass of the sun, however, you would weigh 15 billion tons.

A strong gravitational pull doesn't have to mean that you can't ever get away. If you move quickly enough, you can move away from even a large object. The reason for this is that gravitational pull weakens with distance.

As an object moves away from earth, for instance, the earth's gravity pulls at it, slows it down, and eventually makes it return. If the object moves quickly enough, however, it can get so far from the earth while it is slowing down that the earth's weakening gravitational pull can't quite slow it down all the way. The object keeps moving away and never comes back.

The speed that is needed to get away altogether is called the *escape velocity*.

Rocket

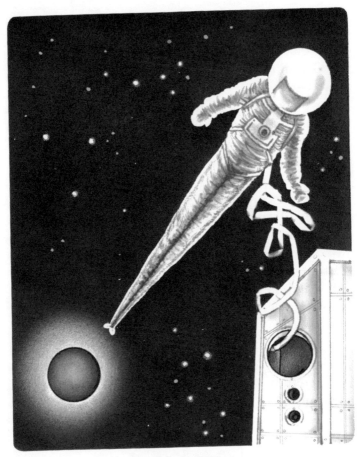

The tidal effect

For the earth the escape velocity is 7.0 miles a second. Any rocket that can reach the top of the atmosphere and is going at a speed of 7.0 miles per second will never return to the earth.

The earth's escape velocity is large, but not too large. We can send rocket ships away from the earth. Larger bodies would be harder to get away from.

For Jupiter, which is a larger planet than the earth and which has a stronger gravitational field, the escape velocity is 37.6 miles per second. For the sun, it is 383.4 miles per second, and for Sirius B, it is 2,100 miles per second.

If we consider a neutron star with the mass of the sun, the escape velocity from its surface is 120,000 miles per second. It would be difficult indeed for anything on a neutron star to get away from its grip.

Light can, though. It travels at a speed of 186,282 miles per second. So do the other radiations that are made up of similar waves but that are longer or shorter in wavelength than light is. Radio waves can get away and so can X rays. That's why we can detect neutron stars.

If you double your distance from the center of any astronomical body, its gravitational pull is cut to one-quarter. On the sun's surface, for instance, you are 432,000 miles from its center. If you moved 432,000 miles out into space, you would have doubled your distance from the sun's center, and the sun's gravitational pull would be reduced to a quarter of its value on the surface.

On the surface of a neutron star, you would be only five miles from the center. At a distance of but five miles above the surface, you would have doubled your distance from its center and its gravitational pull would have been reduced to only a quarter what it was at the surface. The neutron star's gravitational pull drops very quickly with distance, therefore.

Imagine yourself very close to a neutron star with your feet pointing toward it. Your feet would be closer to it than your head would be, so that your feet would feel a stronger pull. The neutron star's gravitational strength drops so quickly with distance that even across the small distance from your head to your feet, the gravitational pull would change noticeably. With your head and feet pulled by different strengths, you would be stretched with considerable force.

This stretching is called a *tidal effect*. This can be felt even with weak gravitational pulls if the object feeling the pull is large enough. The moon's gravitational pull stretches the earth a little bit. Water heaps up a little on the side facing the moon and on the side away from it. This produces the tides, and that is why the stretching is called a tidal effect.

J. Robert Oppenheimer

5 Total Collapse

HOW MASSIVE can a neutron star be? The more massive it is, the stronger the inward gravitational pull. If that gravitational pull gets strong enough, might it not smash the neutrons making up the neutron star? Or can the neutrons stand anything?

This question was considered, in 1939, by the American physicist J. Robert Oppenheimer (OP-en-HY-mer). It seemed to him that the neutrons could *not* stand anything.

If a collapsing object were more than 3.2 times the mass of the sun, then it would not only smash the electrons as it collapsed, it would also smash the neutrons.

What's more, after the neutrons were smashed, there would be nothing else—nothing else at all—that could stop the object from collapsing to zero.

If an object the mass of the sun collapsed, its total

gravitational pull would not change. If you were far away from the collapsing mass, you wouldn't notice any change as the collapse went on.

If you imagined yourself standing on the surface of the mass as it collapsed, though, that would be different. You would be coming nearer and nearer to the center as it collapsed, and you would therefore feel a stronger and stronger gravitational pull.

By the time the mass had collapsed to the white dwarf stage, you would weigh over 1,000 tons. When it reached the neutron-star stage, you would weigh 15 billion tons. As the mass kept collapsing past the neutron-star stage and shrank to nothing, you would weigh more than 15 billion tons—and more—and more—and more.

The tidal effect would become stronger—and stronger—and stronger.

The escape velocity would get higher—and higher—and higher.

The escape velocity is particularly important. As an object collapses *past* the neutron star stage, the escape velocity rises till it becomes greater than 186,282 miles per second. When that happens, light, radio waves, X rays, and similar radiation can no longer leave the object. They don't move quickly enough. Neither can anything else, since scientists are quite sure that nothing can go faster than the speed of light. If light can't escape, neither can anything else.

The distance from the surface to the center, when an object collapses to the point where light cannot escape, is called the *Schwarzschild radius* (SHVAHRTS-shild). It was first calculated by a German astronomer, Karl Schwarzschild.

50

For an object with the mass of the sun, the Schwarzschild radius is about 1.8 miles. It would be 1.8 miles from the surface to the center and then another 1.8 miles out to the opposite surface. That means that if the sun shrank down to a sphere that was 3.6 miles across, keeping all its mass, light could no longer escape from it. Neither could anything else.

Imagine such a small object somewhere in space. Anything that passed close enough to it would be trapped. Tidal effects would pull it apart into tiny fragments. The fragments would circle the small object and eventually fall in. Anything that fell in could never get out.

With things falling in and nothing coming out, the tiny object would be like a hole in space. Because not even light or any other form of radiation would come out, it would seem absolutely black. It would therefore be a *black hole,* and that is what astronomers call it.

A black hole

51

6 Finding Black Holes

CAN WE DETECT a black hole in any way?

If one were close enough to us, we could feel the gravitational effects, but suppose there were a black hole out there among the stars, very far from us. Could we tell it was there?

That doesn't seem likely. A black hole with the mass of the sun would have less than half the diameter of a neutron star. What's more, a black hole would not be sending out pulses of radiation.

With so small a size and with nothing to catch in the way of radiation, how can we possibly detect a black hole?

It might be that we just can't. Black holes may just be something astronomers can talk about without ever knowing for sure whether they actually exist or not.

Fortunately, there is a possible way out. Although

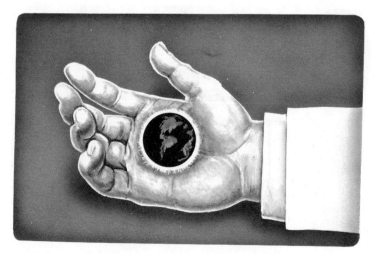

**If earth could fit in your hand
it would be a black hole**

no radiation might come out of a black hole, matter that falls into a black hole would give off radiation *as it fell*. It would give off X rays.

Any small bit of matter that fell into a black hole would only give off a small quantity of X rays. There wouldn't be enough to detect at distances of trillions of miles.

Suppose, though, that there was a great deal of matter falling into a black hole all the time. Then the X rays might be given off in such large amounts that they could be detected.

It does not seem very likely that a great deal of matter would be falling into a black hole. The trouble is that space is so empty. Suppose our sun turned into a black hole. The planets would still circle about it at great distances and would not fall in. Nor would there be much of anything else near the sun to fall in.

But that is because the sun is a single star; it is all alone except for its planets. Nearly half the stars in the sky exist in pairs, however. It is very common to have two stars circling each other, quite close together. Sometimes each star is more massive than the sun.

Suppose we imagine such a pair of massive stars circling each other. The larger one would run out of fuel first, expand to a huge red giant, then explode as a supernova.

The supernova would hurl much of its mass outward, and what was left would collapse into a black hole. Some of the mass tossed outward in the explosion would fall into the other star, which would become much more massive than it was before.

The black hole and its sister star would continue to circle each other. The sister star, more massive than it was before, would now use up its fuel more rapidly and begin to swell into a huge red giant itself.

The outermost layers of the new red giant, on the side facing the black hole, would be pulled toward the black hole by tidal effects. Matter would leak across from the red giant into the black hole, giving up large quantities of X rays as it did so.

This would go on for thousands of years, and during all that time X rays would be sent out into space in every direction, in quantities great enough to detect even at huge distances.

Astronomers on the earth would have to consider the places in the sky where X rays were coming from. If the X rays came from a single point, it would mean they were coming from a collapsed star, either a neutron star or a black hole.

Pairs of stars circling each other

If it were a neutron star, the X rays would be coming out in rapid pulses as the neutron star rotated. If it were a black hole, the X rays would be coming out all the time, for they wouldn't be coming from the black hole but from the material falling into it. In the case of a black hole, the X rays might be coming out in greater and smaller quantities in an irregular way, since at times more matter might be tumbling in and at other times less.

One of the first X-ray sources detected in the sky

was picked up in 1965 in the constellation Cygnus (SIG-nus), the Swan. It was a particularly strong source and was called "Cygnus X-1." When pulsars were first discovered two years later, some astronomers wondered if Cygnus X-1 might not be a pulsar, too, and therefore a neutron star.

Astronomers were just learning about X-ray sources, however, and they didn't have enough information to be able to tell.

Then, in 1969, a special satellite was sent into space with instruments for detecting X rays. The satellite detected and located 161 X-ray sources, and for the first time astronomers had a great deal of material to work with.

By 1971 the instruments on that satellite showed that the X rays coming from Cygnus X-1 varied in intensity in an irregular way. That meant Cygnus X-1 couldn't be a neutron star. Astronomers began to wonder if it might be a black hole.

They studied the place in the sky from which the X rays were coming and discovered that radio waves were coming from there too.

Using both the X rays and the radio waves, the astronomers located the spot in the sky very accurately. It turned out to be very close to a visible star. That star was listed in the catalogues as HD-226868.

HD-226868 is a very dim star because it is very far away. It may be as much as 10,000 light-years away, which would make it about 1,100 times as far as the star Sirius.

Once you allow for that distance, it turns out that the star is a large one with about thirty times the mass of the sun.

Also, this large star is not a single star at all, but is

moving around another star once every 5.6 days. To be making the circle that quickly, the two stars must be quite close together.

The X rays are not coming from HD-226868 but from a spot very close to it. In fact, the X rays are coming from the companion of HD-226868, from the star that HD-226868 is circling.

From the rate at which HD-226868 is making its turn, it is possible for astronomers to calculate that the companion star has five to eight times the mass of the sun.

Red giant in orbit with black hole

Yet when one looks in the place where the companion star must be, there is *nothing there to see.* If it were an ordinary star that was five to eight times the mass of the sun, then it would be bright enough to see in the telescopes even if it were 10,000 light-years away.

Because it cannot be seen, it must be a collapsed star. A white dwarf or a neutron star might not be seen at that distance, but neither a white dwarf nor a neutron star could be that massive without collapsing further.

For all these reasons, many astronomers think that Cygnus X-1 is indeed a black hole, the first to be discovered. There may be many more.

As we have seen, black holes can be formed when stars collapse. Such black holes end up with a mass equal to that of stars and grow constantly as they pick up more and more matter. On the other hand, even small bodies can become black holes if they are pressed together hard enough.

In 1971, an English scientist, Stephen Hawking, suggested that this happened when the universe first began in a "big bang." As all the matter that now makes up the universe exploded, some of the matter may have been squeezed together so tightly in the process that small black holes were formed. Some of those black holes might only have the mass of small planets or even less, and they are called *mini-black holes.*

Hawking also showed that black holes *can* lose mass after all. Some of their gravitational energy is changed into particles outside the Schwarzschild radius and these particles might escape. Such escaping particles carry off some of the mass of a black hole, which "evaporates" in this way.

For large black holes with the mass of a star, the rate at which they evaporate is so slow that it would take many trillions of years for the black hole to be gone. In that time it would gain much more mass than it loses, so actually it would never evaporate.

The smaller the black hole, the faster it would evaporate and the less chance it would have to gain mass.

A really small black hole would lose mass faster than it could gain mass. It would get smaller, therefore, and then it would evaporate even faster and get still smaller. Finally, when it was very, very small, it would evaporate all at once in a kind of explosion that would send out radiation that was even more energetic than X rays. The radiation sent out would be *gamma rays*.

Mini-black holes that were formed at the time of the big bang, 15 billion years ago, might just be disappearing right now. Hawking calculated how big they would have had to be to start with and what kind of gamma rays they would produce as they exploded.

If astronomers could detect just the kind of gamma rays Hawking predicts there should be, that would be good evidence that mini-black holes were formed and that they exist. So far, though, the proper gamma rays have not been detected.

But they might be at any time. And there's still Cygnus X-1.

Astronomers may soon learn much more about black holes and perhaps discover some amazing things about them that will help us all to understand the universe better than we have in the past.

**International ultraviolet Explorer
to monitor energy from the stars**

INDEX